T0195948

SOME CHURCHES HAVE CHAIRS

Written and Illustrated by

ZACHARY C. BRAND

WestBow Press books may be ordered through booksellers or by contacting:

WestBow Press
A Division of Thomas Nelson & Zondervan
1663 Liberty Drive
Bloomington, IN 47403
www.westbowpress.com
844-714-3454

ISBN: 978-1-6642-4516-7 (sc)
ISBN: 978-1-6642-4517-4 (e)

Library of Congress Control Number: 2021919128

Print information available on the last page.

WestBow Press rev. date: 09/28/2021

WESTBOW
PRESS®
A DIVISION OF THOMAS NELSON
& ZONDERVAN

This book is dedicated to you, child of God,
with the hopes that celebrating differences may allow you
to see, experience, and share the love of Christ.

1 Corinthians 12:12-14 (ESV)

"For just as the body is one and has many members, and all the members of the body, though many, are one body, so it is with Christ. For in one Spirit we were all baptized into one body—Jews or Greeks, slaves or free—and all were made to drink of one Spirit. For the body does not consist of one member but of many."

Some churches have chairs.

Kenya - A rural church has people from local villages.
Sometimes, people bring their own chairs to sit on.

Some churches have pews.

Netherlands – A family sits together in a Dutch Reformed
Church. "Reformed" is a type of Protestant Church.

Some churches have bleachers. What does yours use?

Canada- A local school lets the church plant use the gym. A church plant is new church that doesn't have a building yet.

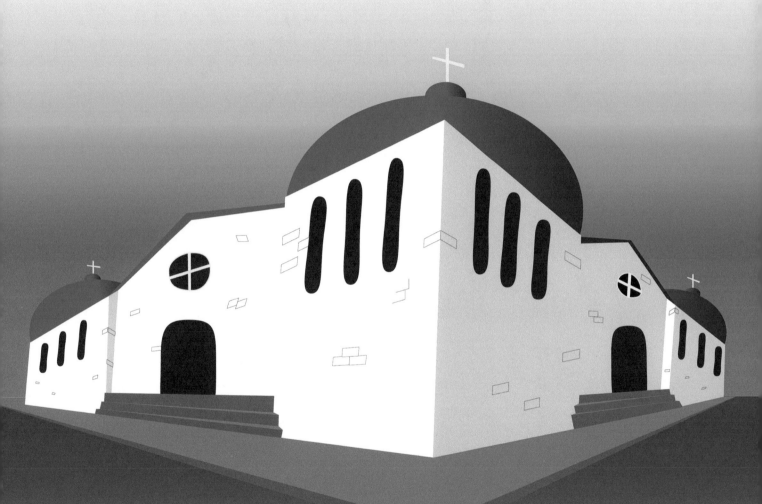

Some churches have domes and bricks.

Greece – A Greek Orthodox Church in the city. The domes remind us that God and Heaven are above us.

Some churches have steeples and paint.

Norway – A Lutheran Church in the countryside. The steeples are very tall so that everyone can see where the church is.

Some churches have stained glass.

Russia – A Russian Orthodox Priest lights candles for worship. The Russian Orthodox cross has two more lines than most other crosses; the top line is for Jesus' nameplate, and the bottom line is for his feet.

Some churches have paintings of saints.

Mexico – A grandmother and granddaughter pray in front of the Virgin of Guadalupe. They are covering their heads with veils, called mantillas.

Some churches have pastors.

America – A Baptist Pastor preaching to the congregation.
"Pastor" is the Latin word for "shepherd."

Some churches have priests.

South Korea – A Methodist Priest prepares for communion. Also called the Lord's Supper and the Eucharist, Jesus gave us Communion as a reminder of his promises.

Some churches have Rabbis (some churches, at least).

Israel – A Messianic Rabbi speaks from the Tanakh, the Hebrew Old Testament. A Rabbi is the leader of a Jewish church, called a Synagogue.

Some churches have choirs.

France – A choir sings during the service. Some people like familiar and reverent hymns called "traditional worship."

Some churches have bands.

Australia – A band plays during the service. Some people like new and upbeat songs called "contemporary worship."

Some dance to the worship.

The Cook Islands — Women dance a traditional dance for Gospel Day, a holiday that celebrates the gospel coming to the islands in the early 1800s.

Christians everywhere lift up their hands.

Some people feel led to lift their hands to God during worship.

Wherever you worship,
whatever you sing,
how ever you praise him,
remember this thing.

We are Christ's body,
and he is our Lord.
We are united
Across the whole world.

Printed in the United States
by Baker & Taylor Publisher Services